Bharat jiva

kari edwards

ISBN: 978-0-9819310-0-5

Original cover collage, "Shadow Buddha," by Fran Blau
Design & typesetting by HR Hegnauer | www.HRHegnauer.com

I gratefully acknowledge the editors of the following publications where sections of this poem have previously appeared: *Moria Poetry, MiPoesias, Tinfish, Black Zinnias, Blueprint Review, Tarpaulin Sky, Horseless Press Review, Otolith, Dusie, Alice Blue, Listenlight, Fascicle, Hamliton Review, Small Town, Sleeping Fish, Private Photo Review, Cabinet Magazine*, and *No Tell Motel*.

—kari edwards

Bharat jiva is made possible by public funds from the New York State Council on the Arts, a state agency, as well as an award from the National Endowment for the Arts. Litmus Press and Belladonna Books are supported by the Council of Literary Magazines & Presses, members, subscribers and individual donors. All donations are tax-deductible.

Distributed to the trade by:
Small Press Distribution
1341 Seventh Street
Berkeley, California 94710

www.SPDBooks.org

Also available directly from the publishers:
Litmus Press | Belladonna Books
925 Bergen Street, Suite 405
Brooklyn, NY 11238

orders@belladonnaseries.org
www.BelladonnaSeries.org

info@litmuspress.org
www.LitmusPress.org

Venn Diagram Productions is the collaborative intersection between Belladonna Books and Litmus Press. This imprint actualizes our mutual commitment to publishing innovative, cross-genre, multicultural, feminist and queer work by writers and artists working beyond and between borders.

A VENN DIAGRAM PRODUCTION | 2009

Belladonna Books Litmus Press

Brooklyn, New York

Bharat jiva

kari edwards

LITMUS PRESS | BELLADONNA BOOKS | 2009

for fran

The will to live is the ground of our existence.
Its negation is our salvation.

—S. Radhakrishnan

oh to be not anyone, gone
this maze of being skin

—Patti Smith

preface

even when issues arise and obedience can not be secured by the bludgeon, the bludgeon remains; when we mention the people, we do not mean the confessional body of the people, we mean particularly itinerant bodies in mechanic flux, preaching freedom beyond flesh pamphlets of authority, concealed in blind devotion. when we mean the people, we mean a people knowing their own strength cast as day laborers, or knowing to a greater part of a lesser known part playing paid intercourse in all connections for the people by the people. when we mean, we mean broke or abrasive worn, once open scream representatives, now incarcerated in a rationalistic shadow land, given a history that merges extruder merchandising with wholesale lots of intermittent dung, or objects for understudy beatings.

it is time to detonate the heart, it's time to call for a sudden and delicious fractal indifference to the written line. no more fail safe dams protecting the audience from exploding stigmatas, tracer bullets and the shit of the dead. it's time for wholesale suicide and redundancy of never going back.

process

somewhere a million times a day, who counts whom, who counts as overlaid texture or mere scenery, counts on a spread sheet that knows no beginning, only newly created zones with mythological plot narratives, about time and always, prescribed by the eternal and immutable moving onward and upwards, forgetting degraded circumstances, undoing the done being before exclusively pitted firm against the sky, glowing sun against linoleum, which bank account hopes property, which bank account gardens growth in the sky of mind?

all this is filtered pools,

the real flatulent affair is

big volume books and tomorrow's thawing

dinner

living that no longer speaks its name

no longer sees itself as anything but

a dish of someone else's amazing burning

figurine.

seeing no reflection in this quasi-nationalistic killing spree and humorless body camp's claim to an address, marching ground for future perfect anti-noise ratio in a box between tao and them, the question arises in a harbor of lies, in an ark with limited thought files, with no hope, but the same. do I choose not to choose and choose drifting beyond greater leisure contacting spirits or eye memory that draws the seasons back, consuming theory intoxicated pain covered with campy fiction, called more real than the real real remains of the day's passive aggressive shallow denial of death's constant face, constant fire, collective scream, covering wounds with vile joviality and expectable performity?

for convenience sake, I accept pasteurized culture in plastic buckets to discover, I wink, I blink, close my eyes for another compliance conflict, pledge of allegiance, skin cover with perishable permanence, keeping one's limbs up and away from lesser bandicoots and reptilian assaults, remembering always the vacant space in front fills with an unseen, unpredictable, absolute this or this collective incompetent translation held in the puppeteer's hands...

the day shifts, we talk to each other the way
we talk to each other, the luster fades, our
bodies fill with sap, there is a shift, joy
reappears before another personal narrative
burns to a heap of citations, continuing in
complicated machinery, becoming blood
knots in space, both the living and dead
surround the present has been. I open my
eyes in the full force of fear and hesitation,
frozen in passing passageways with endless
permutations, subjected to violence, stupidity,
and love.

searching for an endless solution, wanting to denounce tomorrow's demise, something to fill the day's impression, haunted by coarse salt crusted answers, lost singing nothing new, passing through expecting many days ago and many times since. together we watch for snakes and other pests, weather apathy, exchange cautious platitudes amid stick pronouns, search empty ocean remnants in an empty ocean. something kills a passing hope, falls from a building, burns in communal violence, because the morning is "x," caught in "x," resembles plan "x," an incident irritation chained to endless solutions.

can I do this spiritual drag, collective agony wishful thinking, fearful peek-a-boo actuality about to be read in unapologetic disinterested participation against fantasy without benefit familiarity, remembering distortion, forgetting drudgery necessary to consume anything cement sorrow, surrounded by transfer credit surcharge immortal siege ideology, submissive to appliance bodyisms in doubt in the face of stupidity—oops—knowledge, derivative of skin, bone, eyes and the rest, opposite abrupt aggressive remoteness here to serve another ascendant say-so? I tremble in doubt, divided by multiple entry points and explosive content wrapped in rambling overlays sent to the council on commentary, and without exception the animation either frenetic or dull, shifts to no options left, recognizing useless hope in the face of bomb holes caused by numbering digits.

the dream points to glass things, gone and forgotten impossible syllables transplanted nothing empty still in session, pumping blood from disembodied, shrieking, beheaded planted on a pedestal _____ . . . unless contempt rushes in to waste the metaphors, but I am alive in the indescribable, uneditable, ceaseless simply repeated for better national reincarnation about to happen, going on about marriage and love, seeing through someone's saint eternity, repeating words, building walls, claiming doors. this is the land default far from simply erased, being decapitated, leaving letters out, changing thus to "dis," under psychosis. this is proximity land by length and number, where one can maintain death of the self due to lack of a self, referring to another self lost in upstaged tribal purging, pressed fluid and application of details to every detail in heaps of refuse, chanting air hole vastness, forgetting little lungs breathing.

I have to start this again too many times on someone else's planet asking why another noncommunicative withdrawn shadow show, fissures in space, queer in a box brought to tears, knowing how lovely a flower pot on a deck removed for refurbishing can be, stills something sea. maybe again, maybe everyone knows the next move before it happens, otherwise another clay day, starting one forgetting another, twisting unnatural shape for maximum pleasure with no purpose. next week's aromatic extremity mutates to scantly a color beyond black, I speak to a mother about twenty years ago, now and again, twenty years ago, how they die, how they load a gun, how we belong to a warning in the time of security, gray tone with no theme, only moral categorical crimes made up as they happen. trying to fix my attention on what is so rigid to distort the ever changing changeless access apparition of myself drifting in soundless weight, measured by nets, writing fire, erasing the without end.

voices real or imagined attack from the bushes, trailed by night's unspoken full moon imprisoned stereotype, with no deviation in this voiceless humiliation. forced to renounce an absolute on a particular frailty where no source of energy has value, I exist in mass absent lacking, knowing all too well the other existence's living absence seeks incentive acts of perpetual something, created for the theatrical we. subdued, channeled and modified in large part, violence by form by violence of violence, adherence made flesh consumed, protected ledge of human misery, neither renunciate or ghosts, spread through seasons of squalor, given distinction, pathetic wanting and minor mourning.

so nonresponsive our laughter, forgetting it
happens wherever darkness gathers, with
our feet in the rising waters, happening in
relation to opposing terms, mangled
production units meet a system beneath the
tree on the screen in choice situations,
abandoned to bearing nothing outside, on
our backs a happening actual; plotted trees
planned, avenues planted, the harbor
harbors the master's voice of the master's
voice preaching grand review in heavily
scented bottles, our heavenly resale puts the
nail to the nail, wishing searching extended
dreams, stolen eyes wait for happening
words to posit possibility melted in
delightful summa without exception,
happening not enough in terms beyond
utopian insanity, freed from inheritance,
stilled by crushing clouds on a single stem
wet rose.

ready to receive remains built for death, ready to receive the flatly desolate superficial deeply commissioned intellectual offer of suggestive actions, for the hunger assassin to fall back on and become forceful psychological damage, bottled for drinkable agitation.

riding a back seat writing construction, contesting the oncoming molten universe, immersed in villagers, city dwellers, trembling, laughing, (white teeth redone for the perfect test of time), to inhale flesh and stone from long ago, forgetting the horrors of holy oil infusion clocks and gritty body galleries, leaving behind the mourning river's crimson fragrance smoldering from the previous unbearable fever.

in a posture of myself on a speeding body, without hands and feet, I am ready to receive the vomit of consciousness and proceed down the avenues of suggestion to become a limited option.

underneath the haunt ambivalent expenditure, beneath this floor board rental, where boredom is preferred over a discouraging word and the skies darken by day, past little habits and jimmied up smiles, beneath money bodies, rotting fish and scrubbing bubbles, relieved of thinking, sits the foul present, drunk on cheap prayer to a god subdivision.

surrounded by circumstantial sunshine
dog pawing garbage stink
a moon of habits

cluttered with every animal machine guaranteed to revitalize mannerist destiny and take advantage of fetus loving hordes forming cosmopolitan sediment, desperately seeking lottery hackers and a place along the toaster oven set.

doors slam and funnel water phantoms perform surface patricide with limited bandwidth and play vapid absence to things doing things.

guarding against the onslaught of foreign ornamentation, language goods and skin color bar codes; those laid down infringements, designed to not look around or down, so the thinking can be done by another other performing dictionary.

owning the owned, because paper knows best, saying, taste the dirt, this is our land, so chew it up.

in the face of "can't read it," against the
rules of suddenly perceiving enormous
episodes knotted in inexorable reason,
begging cat affection and flash formulas,
those surprise expressions through the
great stream of images, loving the right
place at the wrong time for the wrong
reason, long for another wrong reason
lost place long time lost longing, mulling
exacto knife dollar bills, interpretative
false ideology, drowning complaints,
latent aggressive scenic tedium, and
those hollow tidbit power carnival acts
with their elaborate cotton candy sand for
a two tier body system, otherwise
histories misplaced catatonia undone,
redone, worn down perfect cleansing
acts, by followers and new leased
tongues willing to tell anyone anything
for an otherwise indeterminate seat in
someone's heaven by undoing the done,

must be done for the sake of slash, state, replanted, reworked, broken down homeless exclusive undoubtedly a relative omnipotent great military spring of happiness enacted in the year of law against battered locals without adjectives, living, loving, snuffed out by ready made compositional decrees, inundated by invitation only holiday wage earners seeking another exotic broken into pieces, limitless perceived never anything always more.

I can not take this cold oblivion subterranean vacant surface, sweltering infertility with its sequential token theatrics perform generic guaranteed effects become the cause that causes repeated duplication reissue's imperfect echo with future annotated updates burnish an ever present moment to monumental discomfort pull a kite's string tantrum. and I cannot return strictly speaking, to a time that exists in multiple percentages compounded daily, whether it is a question of passively borne duration subjecting the subject to the best submission desire can order, poked at by remains that devour sensations, or rename suicide publicity stunts interpreted by the passive mangling order as further reasons to disregard another disembodied transposed body, gambled away by artificial green sponges that adorn the garbage heap's violent juices, toxic to any living substance.

I am torn to shreds by an impulse; a sense
of duty that leads everyone to speak on
topics, policy and mean provisions, keeping
all isms to general common sense palette.
according to tradition, the picture
conflicts with the conflict, or the conflict
conflicts with empty organisms and
malleable products.

there are various systems that allow moral
compulsion, derived from overly active
views of perfection, another tradition, a
select few with limited numbered versions,
innately known to the limited numbered
intrinsically determined paths layered in
modified fat truism, that regulate monetary
offerings, religious judgments, or armed
conflict.

the startle response is limited judgment and
becomes irrelevance.

the novel, pre-planned built on a regular past.

after that, after the shards cool and all escape hammerers of metal colored skies, crown the evening affair with still detached mechanically woven sympathy, the weak reason praises the selected imitation, all tenderness is fastened to the assembly line

the wretched are driven to the blinking desert light and slayed for those that speak in celestial darkness.

with the mind I turn towards a vision, a broader encroachment, a particular intensity, veiled distortion and deceitful banking; all for all and nothing for nothing; signs of sudden consumption, fast food learners with dishevelment concrete at the local flavored network, enjoying consumer's delight.

for a while the end is defined by shutting the curtains against deposit receipts, forced labor camps for freedom; the next page shows a parade of bodies and registered trade mark lapses, bargain returns for the dead.

the passion is to protect and defend traditionally conceived lying with acceptable content, gas stations in motion, artillery exploding gloomy waters redesigned for empty heads of brightened desire and total leisure.

the frantic pace is kept; the belief, a floating
condiment stand.

the language, glamorous accumulation
tragedy amid billboards, not unlike the
surface of fences put in place, acquired by
violence.

maintained by force, commissioned by
tradition, or bundles of adrenaline stretched
over denial capital for living.

again, dissemination against encroachment,
against the living, will determine survival
technology for a better attitude, a better
tomorrow to cover the ashes of someone
else's deliverance.

unable to pronounce the word penis due to certain regulatory upstanding back of the throat functions, they build a lake in the desert, wanting to reflect and immortalize immemorial syrup mysticism and break the tongue's will with speech limited virtual obedience.

a million miles from anywhere, taking my body through the days, wondering what all the odd fillings are.

wondering why it is so hard to breathe, as each pore simultaneously defends against and dissolves in a full functioning delusion of tourism never called into question, in an atmosphere of smothering answers made up by the pitifully hopeful and praying arbiters of style.

I watch as we barricade ourselves in and get ready for the unbelievable, unimaginable, unspeakable and unquestioned gender deity of selective speaking to deliver an uncompromising message of the undersigned, replete with regret that other than self-funding fusion that forms a separate self in others, nothing's going to happen sooner than later.

infants rest their face ticks on skeleton mothers. government posters portray effortless generalized scenarios with so called difficulties put to rest. the intended subject fails the mythological word for "once upon a time," nothing specific and there you are, shards of glass and steel in the wind.

the tangible dark seems to come more often.

garments are infected with dropping specifics.

there is nothing else, but reiterative mornings and days with varying permission.

there is a shipwreck on each side of
innuendo, tears gather around the collective
shadow of shadows; none clearer than the
last unshakable, anatomically inexplicably,
never noticed, next time, please sir, more.

enshrouded by fear, one hundred years after
eleven pages of violent reality testing, when
the beginning was the final question, outside
the disruption of anything hungry on
emptiness, suggesting a response of
objections, calling on me to speak in
tongues.

trying to read the consequential future,
apply anything to anything; knowing any
application to the current materiality
is wretched normality and remote
productivity.

yet, after loitering in morning's death, in the
mirror glistening fragrant outside, amongst
mangled bodies and scattered twist ties,
unhealed from unheard names, I am called
back, repulsed, confronted, tormented,
laying in sleeping hands ready to snap.

hives fold into ghettos, the amber sun
disappears where every act is

spoken of in purely stylistic displacements,
reflecting perfect appropriation for
whatever order zone the case may be.
we settle in where the shipwreck is
anatomically inexplicably never noticed
adhering to silent rules in time.

can we have no water on the surface please

no flat moisture

no surface tension;

no zapping starry-eyed dwellers plotting
further absolution

each with their own user friendly light switch
that boasts

clockwork construct allegory

ceaseless mosquito protection

and endless general normal by the standard

set by the character's

imagined generalized apparatus of perfection

fulfilling some higher moral obligation

which nations have embraced

since the earliest days of collective expansion

this is the question of later perfect future

same

sorry, you fail the fingerprint test

no parody deforming equivalent

just controlled sequences

on how many ways a thing can be said

before becoming another ceaseless surrender

to seamless superiority

of the said being restated

with no tension

no zapping restraints

no conceptual consumption

because absolute is absolutely

through the founding glorification lush dangling nonexistence, a speculative utterance falls forth and returns a full figure fist to suppositional nonexistence existence, falls and returns a response to and from, to form a roaring sky, screaming under bush and fierce brambling beast.

maybe a speechless idiot idol, feeling the return, returns to the flesh, something sent through the gate returns hollow, broke, expansive, turned from no longer mind to almost human.

returns again, no longer human, almost mind, teeming commerce, magic hands, ejaculated neighborhoods, space shuttle rabbit-in-the-hat.

the path remains defective perfect, something out of something temporarily

permanent seemingly mythological turned
egocentric logopoesis, plays empire, almost
real, institutionalized salvation, arrested
development.

a figure of speech, returns to its origins,
disfigures force of bramble and fierce excerpt
for nationalistic multiple locations replayed
with instructions.

normal imposed imposes an unexamined
differentiated space, where refiguration is
another remodeled text message memory
card, almost atomic fragment tingle, herding
the blind memory logo complete.

dependent on title deniability

dependent on what system secures what
system

whose metaphysics speaks at lunch for
what interested parties

dependent on who snaps whose gendered
fingers

screams the loudest

incorporates what international code with
internationally recognized trademark,

shifts history to application

plays father knows best without genetic

connective tissue

employs universals without ownership

deploys fill-in-the-blank dream definition
for patriotic employment

for something that works well for the us of
us, defined by us, defined by fill in the
blank static metaphor that shuts down the
power of irony, knows a secret, dies
and gets a thing renamed a thing with a
name.

in the general conservative cast, overcome
by lack of suicidal tendencies, in the worried
beyond reason shaking dense under-growth
invasion of deliberately callous vertebrates,
hotheaded newagers paint possible minds
dirtier than can be produced in a real
whereabouts nonlocation location, crumbling
in darkness.

a breath away from my next instant self,
knowing lies will flow from my lips as well
as the rest; a creative fallacy to create that
which we think we know, with a thousand
pens ready to suggest what one should do.

reminding myself, all ends with what effects
it will have.

reminding myself, all ends with what can be
named and financed, so why not let my
bones be picked by the ants.

reminding myself, I would do anything to not remember who I resemble, I would do anything to not resemble who I resemble, to not resemble the resembled.

reminding my self, I would do anything to not belong to a future human potential workshop, supported by a cast of thousands begging for all things mundane sanity brings, in general overcome by lack of suicidal tendencies.

with a hollow ribcage, my throbbing skeleton continues on an excursionist outside, headlong into an apex of corpses strewn on cash register trail. but first, I must tell you of the million dead children, fast food shrinking bodies, eyes burnt for the privileged and let us not forget, force fed through metal pipes, fattened paté de foie gras. but that is another story, and I must pass onto more plausible explanations by the text, where plausibility is plural in triplicate, with surrender to customs for approval, paid off government officials for expedience, blind eye's turn from the shifting curtain of vital collateral. the throbbing continues, there is a morning call to prayer, an encasement of a village by sound waves, and all this could explain the sequence in various ways; could explain the quest, could explain the novelty, could explain the island episodes with its three part mini-series, or the semi-cultured girl friday volunteer opportunities.

yesterday someone said, someone else called
and left a message, "send your identity, blah,
blah, blah . . . and by the end of the week the
answer will come." so, listen to the rains and
windmill or something like that. the question
will have to wait, blah, blah, blah . . . the truth
is variable, comes in grams and kilos, and
splendor will fall on castle walls, crumbling
with age and arrogance, en masse on the
battlefield surrounding hunks of decay, in
echoes of dying, blow-by-blow they fall, life
piled on life, so on and so on and so it goes.
the answer varies under severe torture, some
feel no pain, while others go shopping and die,
blah, blah, blah . . .

. . . or as an alternative ending, though I cannot see you, I say to you in great humility, you cannot do anything for us or me or them. we become unclean the moment you enter our lives . . . no more relief, no more public education. asking us to remain motionless with our wings folded, waiting for obliteration and nuclear extinction, while soil grows in test tubes having already destroyed everywhere else. no, the answer does not judge between the catalog of truths, simply stages them in separate spaces. this is not science fiction, more dumbstruck withdrawal, blah, blah, blah . . . because truth can not be stored in strategic segregation, proclaiming opposition where there is complicity, denying possible randomness, because we do not seek the essence of contact, but look only for the effects to match our a fill-in-the-blank escape medium impressions, blah, blah, blah . . .

being able to only harness life through dead words, what do I know of surpassing this itinerary of madness; by rote, a reiterative condition full of dull terror; by arrogance of mind, accumulative sins, tears, idle tears, and divine tears of despair? and in the morning darkness and in the distance without a pool to cast a reflection in even, only odds and ends of text to read through, wallowing a body, where behind each act is a play in which one can choose to be one of three characters in the royal family, or the chameleon eating bugs on the road side, dodging the hordes on the way to low calorie enlightenment. or could it be a david before growing to a goliath or frankenstein's monster who bases all on paradise lost's ruined offspring and universal blank? my mind runs amok in the rains and rumors of rat eating vipers. some say, "celebrate the small things," in relation to what? nothing? two point perspective or multiple worlds emerging, leaving one in a myriad of infinite undulating unimaginables?

some of the glories sigh for prophets
some sigh and take the cash
shed a silken tear
for those buried alive

one-by-one
scattered on the ground
too minuscule to nourish
licking the soil
hoping for proof-of-proof
to nurture swollen bellies
mixed with fecal matter and cast-off flesh

a lamp amid darkness
on lips of poor fruitless attempts
secret dreams dream of
heavenly vintage tomorrows
and a cup of dust carcasses

running sadness to the ground
divided
running sadness to the ground
strange though
I prefer to play with matches
rough ride midnight's helpless plea
under yesterday's lapse into
praying for an evolutionary jerk forward

oh body
washed in blood
and covered in phosphorous ash
spring me one last breath
filled with real remnants
quicksilver and lead
let me drink from your
sorry scheme of things

let me touch the spot
that bites back

I lost my place in a double action mixed
    anthropomorphized metaphoric whoops
knowing what is is knowing what is is is not
    seen
those few original experiences driven hard into
    soft pockets of flesh
lost in a cabinet of song creatures
mocking accidental intermission generators
labor acquiring please please place me in a
    stone body
beyond longer lost deferment insufficiencies
where extension phones form births of
    forgetting
weddings and funerals, mourning and festivals
tear rocks on lost cliff legs
time-mirage accents conveniently indivisible in
    units of salt
somewhere where light is law
evaporates pure reason

behind the divided division, beyond the dissolution
somewhat nothing phenomena, dividing infinite
division, washing over phantasmic arcane
subordinate clauses, washing over plasma, washing
infinitesimal monstrous possibilities in continuous
byproducts, by the dozen, permanent manners,
semi-permanent never permanent sorting, sorting
wet rocks from wet, getting ready to feed the
hungry, dividing words dividing lines into lines,
dividing rose from air, form from rose, air from a
photograph of someone I never knew, from
someone I will never know, dissolving something
wasting away, something wet, something rock, lost
dissolving, talking to who is talking to who is you,
to see how much sees how much time divides,
constantly dividing counting verbal slippage, action
theory, a story line in time, cost per million, per
head, per grain of sand, a point in case in a point
time . . . pure and applied, seemingly recast mis-
spoken, speaking seemingly, always on time,
opposed to those mute struggling, hungry, buried,
rolling military nights, rolling new highways, new
ways to count sweetness, dividing lies by stains,
removing eyes for truth's sake.

let's get serious, say goodbye, have a good time,
say so long, someone has to die, someone has to
display our short term collective grief, with no
mention of single issue essentialist politicians,
going on and on about wonderless glories and the
many second or third rate comings, falling in and
out of fashion, in and out of time, in a service of
"truth," to another so on and oh so perfect
mother and father extension.

so, let's get personal and wonder, are more books
coming, waiting for more of the same, waiting
while long neck gods talk to short legged pigs,
while the pigs talk to the horses, and the rest
watch mysterious shadows making mysterious
animations without hands, waiting for the
rapture.

happy one moment, dead the next. sometimes
hungry, a moment later starved to death on fat.
the divine majority chants certain cathedral tunes,

internal difference becomes a thing, to a thing in a holding cell, sealing imperial fears, disregarding the deadened landscape, unable to breathe, meeting machinery conceptions of absorption bodies, impressing mind machines working with corporal mentality on the surface everything.

so, let's get serious, say good-bye, wait for another on-time A-bomb, cut off, collectively lost, as long as you believe in, as long as you think, as you believe in thinking in believing in . . . click your heels, repeat after me, though I can not represent myself, we must represent the not representative whole impossible to represent.

so, let's get personal, get serious and translate violence into another form into another place in time, before the majority sings moral creation songs in the celestial cathedral till dawn . . . let's get personal, say good-bye, I love you, someone has to die.

there must be a crazy power, intermittent instruments, and or a chain of water, unchained, rippling full, while others drop away. I think flashing panoramas, a natural harbor steeped in the sun's implicit staying, firm ballooning speechless jest, tittering momentarily there. someplace not rip-tooth skyline frozen acetate. someplace obscure. someplace not a prophet's immaculate condensed reality, enforced by pliers, plagued by an outside outside, grabbing disappearing starlight. there must be a world of words, uncentered decay, light penetrating flesh to bone, without a conveyor belt construct, mapping another absurd rational predicament something unfurnished, not already saturated with history's whispering sloganisms. someplace the foot falls, surrounded in a medium, clearly falling, falls clear, gives way to conscious ramifications of disremembered walking, falls forward from the flowing lamp towards dawn's supplement of love. there must be a dawn somewhere flashing quick, not plagued by decay and too many billowing words.

trinity has been illuminated, the water
poisoned, timetable spies are at each corner
and there is trouble in paradise; wisdom
quits, shut out again, and again. we have
reductio ad absurdum, repeating violent
paradoxes by stunning thought's antithesis,
forgetting it is the passage, not
accumulation. repeating how can one,
within a context, flesh-out wild speculation,
before and after the beginning, now, forever
and beyond that which can never be
described? each with its own effect, that
effects the effect, an undefined rhythmic
whole, predetermined without an original
inherent end and or beginning, sending
something mind longing for euphoric
postcard perfection, waiting for whatever,
claiming mind, nothing but mind, claiming
something fluid; geography bodies, surface
probabilities, anti-accumulation procedures,
sugary eruptive tectonic vibrations,

dwindling fenced voices without broadcast torment, mountains of neatly stacked lumber burn counter lollipop paws, not regulated according to some measured sound, divisible by a sentence, exchanged for points in space, worked out in advance, is a result of . . . that is in relation to . . . whose war is . . . whose lite heaven receives the most sponsorship in anticipation of g.o.d.s

limited engagement, for those believing in air conditioned patterned polyester, plastic wrapped rubble by the second, burying the dead and tirelessly speeding away.

the complaints keep piling up, I count 12 x 12 x 12. it is another world's world, writing blank blank about blank, getting blank complaints about blank x 12 x 12. So, let's begin with a place ideal, something idyllic ideal, 12 x 12 a place space, static pileup, human and non-human compilation merge through detour psychic cartography and non-qualitative personalities; metric objects, by lack of rigor. interior forms emerge by document worn blank, suffused by 12 x 12 complaints, about blank something ideas or ideals. there in fundamental errors in fundamental human non-human static thought form interchange, in the original statement, in the incapacity, and impotencies, fortifying self limitations, opaque overpayments for import / export convulsions, returning immortality to immediate panic energy surcharges, x 12 x 12 blank piles-up, crashes mad hatter into judgment hour, fails to acknowledge the vast two handed machine, the beginning place complaint machine, without the question, "how did this produce a normative blank times blank, with a lack of psychic documentation x 12?"

often secret lover's
walled limits
place the mouth
or wound
at the water's edge

narrows led
somewhere
with nothing to give
nothing to learn
just abundance
reminders of opulence

and degradation
dog territory
with too much
repetition of another
other
almost same
teetering edge

enough for half an arm
and distorted legs
crawling begging
faded halftones
muted indigos
deaf crimsons
cracked and moldy ochre
to reflect decay
in a dialogue of warmth

waking up after waking up

after another artificial anti-depressive smile

wakes up individually wrapped cheese

freezing not unlike a lisp

stammering and stuttering to stay warm

uncountried, constantly under flag

freezing trying to wake up

flanked by

freezing heads in cars

bodies in malls

stammering house moments

stretched form from here to

freezing next to the next

individually wrapped

ignored historical doritos nacho cheese

cool ranch next to

doritos reduced fat nacho cheesier

flavored next to the natural white nacho

cheese

next to 50 kinds of frozen fragments

waking up

frozen for more time

more cheese

barely warm

badly blurred homeless

positions away from action

individually stammering

articles on freezing

not word boxes

fill in the blank

not so much capital

crumbling cracking

bigger broader sucking wounds

crumbling walls

sucking air

and frozen cheese

please no more answer thing pleasure in the billion word nothingness life universal proposition prayer thing, sitting in nothing, doing nothing all day long, hoping for anything pleasure land right there on your door step unannounced.

please no more over greatness with an ever over greater over greater apparatus box stuff game, getting bigger than big, every day reflecting flicker mind, on and off every second second.

please, please try to remember to refuse the surface response memory of the all-in-all thing code dog cow grazing in the midday sun shining off the nonattachment grass, that happens only once in a lifetime, to become a memory photo essay this side of a poem, in the hall of everything, going faster than nowhere.

so let us stop, for a moment and listen to
the sharp triangulation in unheard still winds
remembering the earth's primordial cry,
orbit the next day's dream eruption,
reflecting light time, water time, and the first
day landing on land time, going slow,
breathing hard, passing quickly to genocide
epistemology held in collective paragraphs,
marking other's parentheses, forgetting
everyone's hand is on the machete, just to
prove it can be done again and again.

and again in the usual word place, can we
please, please, watch the thing that slowly
breaks the finger, moves along the body,
records codes, repeats to someone for some
kind of salvation? there is no other question,
other than the one hundred billion billion
billion continuous conditions bemoaning the
heart, lung, body, held together in the
morning quarrel, cool misty pasture, trying

to find the pleasure in everything moment,
right there laying on the street staring to the
sky, waiting for someone, anyone to put
their starvation hand in my face, to pay
attention to anything right now, thank you.

someone said
could not happen

it happens
a million times
happens
someone dies
a million times

our tupperware atmosphere dies
without fear or thought
twilight dims
hatchback idealism
bounces from ouija board
to zodiac killer
from I ching to magik 8 ball

yes, we have a winner

miracles today

call 1-800- complete resignation

drunk banality

prays for insight

anything to stop this

crown of thorn conquest

happening

nobly and remote

keeps happening

canned in cigarettes and ice investments

for a future shipped

orgy of dead animal remains

standing in a vague burning

terrified unstable

exposed to a potential body, exposed constantly exposed, broken to bits to prove death's limits, choosing the most logical answer, someone said, "do not do this." someone else said, "do not presume screaming one more time will prove anything," will divert broken bodies to bits, to form another lonesome particle of something between multiple co-authored epics and another official counter-sentence, grotesquely misplaced, measured in the name of . . . blown to bits to prove, wounded by bullets, disfigured by rumor, crippled by falling lies, in a state of the state of euthanasia, choosing the most logical question to prove, what is the correct program? what is the correct proportion of rice? and what is that something between partition and pogrom? what is that something piles in vain, tears in suits, linked to fantasies hidden blindness, full of strife and bitter endings? what is a body that can be a body not constantly exposed, blown to bits?

I can not begin to know

producing difference by deferring

second third person construction

in the first third person narrative

promising surrender to the dead

acknowledging, I am an unknown participant

something maybe, something blind

consuming scarcity

producing hunger

constructing gender

breathing markers

making someone a thing

scapegoat instance

another perfect occasion

construct of a common sense sentence

out of many different bank accounts

apparently to produce

a final outcome

illumination legible

newspaper flyspeck

on the edge of an abstract noun

sliding affirmation

speaking of poverty

in an industrial world

where the lakes, rivers and oceans

are no longer lakes, rivers and oceans

but mud covered hunger living in bodies

this resort moon

stalks our lavishness

calls down the involuntary

only to crash through

oncoming mental grids

roars past nothing

past a thousand petal laughter

children's caricatures of angels

turned fowl

turned fool

turned carnivorous

a bed

an absence

and how did this

sudden change

from curiosity to aggression

tempt all

with emancipation and joy

reviewed by another madness

devouring its own

fabulous song

in scorching heat?

something fails to realize, something casts
another other opaque profit
bloom elsewhere. I ask someone for
more time in a field of time, where
there is a choke hold on language, in
the masses, in the throat, in a gag reaction,
in the unbroken yesterday, today, and
tomorrow. afraid to
speak to something anything,
fearing the fear of fear, afraid to
speak to tell-tale hearts turning to
something rewritten to too many
forgotten mistaken, rewritten times. to
be sure, someone invades the
margins, secures the premises,
quotation marks disappear and
reappear. everyone attempts to
guess who is looking under what
underneath layer of flesh. the many
missing, impossible possible, over-
determined nonbelievers,

acknowledge the road does not exist,
the line does not exist, forever is
forever broken, never a conduit for
listening. our blood is your blood,
our house is your house, listening
for another exit possibility to exist,
in another other's cry for love,
bleeding tears for the many. and as
sure as no reason answers an answer
answers, daylight becomes night,
calling it, library card liberty,
sacrificing the lower part for
plunder, until one discovers no
other issues, carried in pre-thought
pleasure on wings inside smile, in
the slow unseen deck of nature's
obedience.

if beyond the self is the self, is the self beyond essential multiworld universal non-escapable caring, curious, multiple wave forms snaking sensual manifestation of another walking talking piece of praying salvation childhood romp in a field, not quite a field, expanding rough hewn physical expression of momentary dream centers, centered in that that has no center, transforming harmony to a determinate other, to another succession of overlapping finite appearances, appearing for the first time beyond anything and fully present in a dying mumbling prayer, thrown to the next baptized wayward fringe of a pale afternoon opportunity, dumb with luck quivering conscious incantation, sensing joy, sorrow, pleasure, pain, truth, error, good and evil, dissolving over the moment, forming an egocentric appendage realized in transmutable variables, sending and receiving to a self that has no center, only moments of semi-aquatic lucidity.

left amongst crumbling and abandoned dogs
sacred cows, o'henry and shakespeare
left amongst tagore and fashion magazines
left amongst the unpacked, redistributed
and subdivided

left in the lightness of street cracks
packed in something and everywhere
one time is not another time
it's all the time
backing into a makeshift universe
complete with infinity and sunlight

shifting centrifuge in straightjacket ease

a blue modeled shiva

dark illuminating

holy cows, goats, and beggars,

millions doing everything

shifts into view

a plaster order comes to order

above a something for everyone

doing a job

that was then now, a newer

    that was then, now

more of the same only more

    with each step an increase

stuff in the cracks

something order called to order

    called to prayer

chaos bodies beyond physics

proving something semi-real not recognizable

other world walls of bodies

    a street of bodies

a street of everything
bits and pieces form a universe of things
no holes just parts and pieces of parts
unconnected ghost heads, remnants of millions
chant nothing but god
    for the birds in distress
    and the one-legged beggars
harm nothing do nothing come to prayer

everyone's dying
everyone's dying to die
everyone's in my way
on my way to die
it's too hot and dusty to die
I am eating the ashes of the dead
eating the exhaust of cars
an image sacrifice
looking for a boat to heaven
namaste,

your boat has bad karma

out of the way

I am burning inside of shame

I am at the seat of the ash

on a boat to nowhere

burning inside

I am the end of time

shiva orange

rat queen

goddess of money

sleeping in time to die at the hands of doms

sunrise to sunrise from the beginning of time

alone at the end of time

rowing nowhere

lost in serpentine alleys

amongst the amputees and water buffalos

amongst dust breathing souls

looking into eyes

looking back

for anything

not burning

in another reality   the choking begging
reality   the soft porn deformed
filling the cracks with a human ocean
consumed in a single serving   etceteras
and bleeding   cockroach consumption
breathless and again   the future is here
again and again   the picture is mad
gnaws at the self   confronting a wall of
oncoming traffic mercenaries   with
habitual disregard   for things and bodies
a sensation rekindled in filth   line the
causeways to a choking point

a minute ago   swallowed by
a slow inward mute   demonic world
countless crawling faces   unable to speak
sheared off at the lips   a
deflected possible   a mathematical
probable   a bride to a new moral
code   in another reality   already here

the word "seemingly," in the last sentence, is "seemingly" supreme. the syllables are but fast food and death, a condiment that "seemingly" contains time marvels and theological puns atop syringe intellect, in the dungeon of the heart, "seemingly," at the center of accumulation self-esteem. light comes through glasses of a different color, without "seemingly" to be anything other than light, never accumulating, never clinging, "seemingly" for eternity.

oh, ship of sleazy bliss

rose-red glasses

please light my   iridescent self control

please please

give me

optionless pre-packaging

once again

oh, ship of rose-red

crushing sleaze

please   light my durable options

and choke my editorial domination

is nothing supposed to be nothing

doing, I suppose

it could be anything

preferring the other's teeth

keenly aware of   days later

two places at the same time

doing jackal ambiance

suffering

the three miracles of anticipation

doing all that can full throttle antagonism

later, only to dissolve in whatever winds

ending ATM blessing rates

reassessing the self

delighting the self and making art respectable

whose   mind   thinks   thinking   body   tongue

speaking

whose tongue   whose eyes

whose ear of ear

thinks body   tongue

speaking speech   eye of eye

of that that   cannot be

of whose mind   thinks

can only be seen

spoken of   by the tongues

breathless breath

unheard from dawn

in the fire wind lightning

motion in the mind

two trembling minds face each other

through a mass of hallucination

held together by a series of obligations

beyond the 16 part universe

beyond the nothing held together   left

undone

the thief   no longer the thief

murder no   longer murder

in a blank hour past a mood

that stood by speaking sense

beyond this and that and everything

beyond relationships

ever changeless   web of spiders

beyond attempting to speak a victim's

own mythological motif

a place where fat melts

beyond

this and that and everything

burns a formula

born imperishable
blazing two minds
a bed of flowers
trembling indecipherable

so, put some salt in water, wait till morning
wait in the mind
that waits in words
arrives in the wait

put some salt in the mind
taste the morning waters
in the will
that puts salt in the mind

concentrate nothing
before salty water
reflect the joy of instantaneous rest
in the continuum
of verbs, nouns, and adjectives
after the point and comma

listen to the sound waves

take the breath away

swell from salts

watery everything

pronounce a body

covered salt

dwelling empty

reflect indestructible matter

unkempt by anyone

buried beneath

bodies saline reflection

I'm flying nonstop for six months   at 2,057,152
yojanas per second   to escape   the
suffering inside tires   the california talk of
suicide   and the many things from which no
one benefits

I do not have a name for it   one hundred times a
day   I do not have a name for it   when your
fearful mouth smashes heads against teeth   and
against the streets

it could be there are the seven boundaries   seven
truths   and the ancient vigor of cows

it could be   interested in history   used a
recorder   in two too many closets   spoke
to the stone   that spoke to the stone, etc...

and it could be   there is not there here   at the
intersection of   wounded traffic   burrowing
lights into   twisted extraordinaire   borderline
intelligence   established in the   dull never
mind of time   with its all too familiar
domestic touching

without a second
deep within vast separate
nothing porous
river rising
consumed by flames
a body instant
before
the instant expires
something
witness
nothing further
through fire
to perceive another other

                                  rubbed in syllables
                                          like oil
                                       like butter
                                       like water
                                     like a photo
                              freed of its image

in some ways
I am afraid
I've been someone
in a headache of dust
not adept at advocating for others
transpiring away in crevices
between smithereens and darkness,
where I grasp
pronoun logic
the texture of cement
a b-side on repeat
with a skip
at best

a disassociation of matter

sinking profoundly in sinking progress

preparing to enter a nothing more

present dark above

clutching the hand

of unconsciousness

without a name

one accumulates

in the dreams of the 84 fools

beyond deeds

breathing in

the breathing universe

breathing unseen dark matter

breathing through membranes and energetic

ellipses

cascading off the solar plexus

off the ocean tides

off the condensation
on the window pane

with a name steadfast
adrift in the fires of time
in the morning furies of birds
in the nakedness of raw poverty
in every word ever spoken
flowing inexhaustible
sacrificial attention
all seventy-two thousand
never endings
dreaming dreams
that dream dreams

ordained hunger
alone in slaughter
working the soil
legs walk
a road behind

those who speak
a voice without hands
scattered upon
surface rotation

it's not for the
table of contents
motives
desires
or grande
total results

it's not for
the glorious manifestations
liquid arenas
endless realities
sliding across
both hemispheres

it's for those moments

less than shame

proclaim difference

surging sounds

a sentence later

examining

a previous

unknown missed manifestation

it could be

forgetful days

performing mountainous situations

a bowl of soup

blood dripping fingers

twilight

the smell of another

who knows the other

who is neither not this

or not that

or not another

it could be

incomprehensible

drawing one near

a ruinous state

and letting it happen

it could be

honey bearing

intelligent rumor

droplets of water

breathing air

being the air

between lightning

and lingering thunder

held together

by burning droplets

today's the day
the earth stood still
today I sat in 700 directions
screaming monkeys
coughing hacking
general medieval milieu
of propaganda

today we all die
wake-up
and die again

today the moon
sun, stars
polar ice caps melt
the ice cream melts
the tv melts

today we are told we have 26 years to live
today I watch the cement crumble
juxtapose love with everything

even doubt

build walls faster than regulatory principles

today is the day before we die

waiting an agenda

watching the walls fall

chained like dogs

offering up fire resistant

sense delighting

surface stings

many crested

100 times sagas

fearless ready to die

asking for nothing

on what the sky paints

in pollen left from history

lion hue phosphorescence

of monosyllabic silent slant

repetitive trees

first forest vowel

compounds time

and it flowers

behind luminous curtains

corners away from death's ledge

between stones and ceaseless

lips covering another's

discovering small nothing wrong

shedding salt

amidst another's

petal that sheds

shifting breeze

bound by a hundred times

a thousand times

derived from nothing

steeped in clouds, sky,

water and fire

if the body dissolves
to a spotless sphere
if all I can do is
a series of incidents
lost in mathematics
withdrawn to obtain a body
that remains a desolate vagrant
if longing for a name,
shelters an ocean
a hundred and forty suns
set a blaze
dissolvable and indivisible
if out of the unreal comes
divisional smooth traveling
bound motionless totality
far below the senses
far below the knees
waging mimic dazzle
flash statements made
if nothing and nothing
again

did I not say to you

did I not say

they will implant ugly qualities

did I not say

saying something

eager to die into the deathless

did I not say

have you heard

the silent steps

innermost names weeping

did I not say

in the pangs of separation

world-filling light

running through our veins

saying

I must leave

the earth in a mind without fear

did I not say

raised an acrobat

on the clumsy ground

in the dirt

on an organ

while the puppets

danced above

did I not say

like a wedge

in a block

yea, a thing

did I not say

life can get tired of living

living another insisting babylon

did I not say

despite the body

there is a universe

despite the universe

born waves of existence

did I not say

saying I must go

did I not say

death does not annihilate particles

it only breaks up conjunctions

did I not say

gone ready to depart

distortion grammar
here talking of changing
only to history

at times adrift
    inside drowsiness
    above tombs and bricks

at times released by the stomach and teeth

at times released by something struggle
    realized adrift in abiding nothing

at times static
    released of human personality

at times beyond description
    round and empty

at times dead and buried
    spectacle suffering opposites

at times ecstasy and wordless

at times inside a stone heart burning
existence
    neither delight or aversion
    no difference between a thing

at times with untethered remains
 thick and guttural
    remembering thought bodies
    and thoughts of thoughts

at times common meaning
    with seal of joint consistency

the fire confronts its wetness
confronts land that trembles
at the front of
earth bound thoughts
thinking cockroach pause
resignation
knocked dead by soldiers
moving grief
condition pretend
fearing intoxication
ecstasy of the marvelous
eternal obedience to love
instead we stand
drunk at the gateway of ants
a hulking mass
of rock imperceptible
intimidation on a metal surface
sleeps perpetual
abrupt empty

deaf to

rhapsody's murmur

splendid boundless laughter

nothing shatters space

like the imagined real

disturbing regularity

with its regular

promising something

like a real show

nothing gathers up stones

replaces them with shadows

replaced by space

containing neither

proposition or time

nothing left

passing blossoms

sweet perfume

betrays a secret

kisses your feet

and clings to nothing

who will finally complete themselves

to not exist

to see the unseen of the unsaid

in the book of nothingness

that began before birth

who will everything everyone

happening in blood and urine

whose content is not reiterable

who will be the first to quit talking
in intimate unfolding

who can contain enough
without augments of brick and mortar
who without supplement of names and
numbers

who under terror of gasoline
will meet the leopard and attack the trainer

who will only desire
fusion
with the rains
dripping rhythm
demand a moment
of your time

who will
awash within a stream
of distractions

spill without reference
on to text of tradition
mixed with subtropical blue mist
and the vacuum of space
happen with corporal clarity
carnivorous and wet
steeped in a powdery light thought
that thought everything without sunrise

aftermath

nothing to say any more,
expelled from injured paradise
incarcerated in plural driven substitutions

nothing to imagine anymore,
given another calmer euphemism
left blank for another weak absurdity

nothing to say any more,
seeking urgent home serving as body and
limbs,
further on; drama and numbers, dead leaves
and twigs

the exercise book reads
permanently wrenched from a swarm of
messages
undone, replaced by a generous claw with
nothing to say

in the low brown out a pattern appears,
flat conformist appendage
weak link to limitation
a self contained comical system
offering leverage suicide
an aberration with intolerable delirium

it taunts with a succession of proofs and
irresistible lies

whose house swarms with rats
coming from whose faces
whose words
only offer momentary purity for a bitter
end
where nothing is true and all is false

Bharat — a republic in the Asian sub-continent; second most populous country in the world; achieved independence from the United Kingdom in 1947.

jiva - living spirit.

green
press
I N I T I A T I V E

Litmus Press and Belladonna Books are committed to preserving
ancient forests and natural resources. We elected to print this
title on 15% post consumer recycled paper, processed chlorine
free. As a result, for this printing, we have saved:

2 Trees (40' tall and 6-8" diameter)
856 Gallons of Wastewater
1 million BTU's of Total Energy
52 Pounds of Solid Waste
178 Pounds of Greenhouse Gases

Litmus Press and Belladonna Books made this paper choice be-
cause our printer, Thomson-Shore, Inc., is a member of Green
Press Initiative, a nonprofit program dedicated to supporting
authors, publishers, and suppliers in their efforts to reduce their
use of fiber obtained from endangered forests.
For more information, visit www.greenpressinitiative.org.

Environmental impact estimates were made using the Environmental Defense
Paper Calculator. For more information visit: www.papercalculator.org.